D0122124

CALGARY PUBLIC LIBRARY

JUL   2011

This book

_____

_____

_____

Written and compiled by Sophie Piper
Illustrations copyright © 2011 Elena Temporin
This edition copyright © 2011 Lion Hudson
The moral rights of the author and illustrator
have been asserted
A Lion Children's Book
an imprint of

Lion Hudson plc

Wilkinson House, Jordan Hill Road,
Oxford OX2 8DR, England
www.lionhudson.com
ISBN 978 0 7459 6260 3
First edition 2011
1 3 5 7 9 10 8 6 4 2 0
All rights reserved

Acknowledgments

All unattributed prayers are by Sophie Piper and Lois Rock, copyright © Lion Hudson.
The prayer on page 30 by Victoria Tebbs is copyright © Lion Hudson.
Bible extracts are adapted from the Good News Bible, published by The Bible
Societies/HarperCollins Publishers Ltd, UK © American Bible Society 1966, 1971,
1976, 1992, used by permission.
The Lord's Prayer (on page 61) from *Common Worship: Services and Prayers for the
Church of England* (Church House Publishing, 2000) is copyright © The English
Language Liturgical Consultation, 1988 and is reproduced by permission of the
publishers.

A catalogue record for this book is available
from the British Library
Typeset in 14/20 Elegant Garamond BT
Printed in China November 2010 (manufacturer LH06)
Distributed by:
UK: Marston Book Services Ltd, PO Box 269, Abingdon, Oxon OX14 4YN
USA: Trafalgar Square Publishing, 814 N Franklin Street, Chicago, IL 60610
USA Christian Market: Kregel Publications, PO Box 2607, Grand Rapids, MI 49501

Prayers
For All
Seasons

Sophie Piper ★ Elena Temporin

LI🐻N
CHILDREN'S

Contents

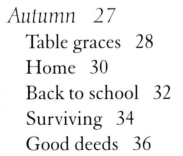

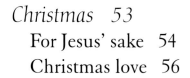

Spring

Thank you, God in heaven,
For a day begun.
Thank you for the breezes,
Thank you for the sun.
For this time of gladness,
For our work and play,
Thank you, God in heaven,
For another day.

Traditional

Springtime praises

Bless the Lord of heaven above,
sing to God with thanks and love.

Praise him for the joyful spring,
bringing life to everything.

Praise him for the blossom trees,
birds and butterflies and bees.

Praise him for the cloud and rain,
and for sunshine once again.

Bless the Lord of heaven above,
sing to God with thanks and love.

Glimpses of heaven

The wild birds are calling out
their wild morning song
to praise the Maker God
to whom all wild things belong.

Thank you for the little things
we notice every day
that shine on earth
with heaven's gold
and cheer us on our way.

Rainbow promises

Rainbow reaching up so high:
may the sun shine in the sky.

Rainbow reaching to the ground:
may the rain fall all around.

As the seasons come and go,
may God bless this earth below.

May the springtime seeds unfold;
may the harvest ripen gold.

Summer

Let me drift like a seagull
up in the summer sky
feeling the air grow gold and warm
as the sun rises high.

Let me drift like a seagull
out on the sea so wide
feeling the ocean rise and fall
as the moon pulls the tide.

Let me drift through summer
down by the ocean shore
marvelling in God's creation
now and for evermore.

Holidays

I love to have sand between my toes,
to watch the tide as it comes and goes,
to pick up shells and throw them away:
thank you, dear God, for my holiday.

O God, you have counted each grain of
    the sand
  and the shells that lie washed on the shore.
Please keep us all safe, as if holding
    your hand
  through this day, through this week,
    evermore.

17

Creatures of the deep

Lord of the ocean,
Lord of the sea:
Let all the fish swim
Strong and free.

Lord of the wavetops,
Lord of the shore:
Keep them all safe
For evermore.

Birds and flowers

God feeds the birds that sing from the treetops;
God feeds the birds that wade by the sea;
God feeds the birds that dart through the meadows;
So will God take care of me?

God clothes the flowers that bloom on the hillside;
God clothes the blossom that hangs from the tree;
As God cares so much for the birds and the flowers
I know God will take care of me.

Based on the words of Jesus

Bright and beautiful

All things bright and beautiful,
All creatures great and small,
All things wise and wonderful,
The Lord God made them all.

C. F. Alexander (1818–95)

He prayeth best, who loveth best
All things both great and small;
For the dear God who loveth us,
He made and loveth all.

S. T. Coleridge (1772–1834)

Outdoors

Thank you, dear God,
for the deep brown earth,
and the rippling grass so green.

Thank you, dear God,
for the high blue sky
and the wind that blows all unseen.

Autumn

The harvests have ripened in the sun;
There's plenty of food for everyone:
There's some for ourselves and more to share
With all of God's people everywhere.

Table graces

The bread is warm and fresh,
The water cool and clear.
Lord of all life, be with us,
Lord of all life, be near.

African grace

For health and strength
and daily food,
we praise your name,
O Lord.

Traditional

Let us take a moment
To thank God for our food,
For friends around the table
And everything that's good.

Home

Dear God,
May we make our home a place of love and
kindness for all. May we share the things we
have with generosity and cheerfulness.

Victoria Tebbs

30

A prayer about my family,
for, though we all are odd,
we love each other very much:
for this, I thank you, God.

31

Back to school

Dear God,
Help me as I learn new things.

When I learn quickly and easily, may I help others
to understand.

When I make mistakes, may I find out what went
wrong and put things right.

Help me never to be afraid of new things, but
to see them as an adventure.

Bless to me, O God,
the work of my hands.
Bless to me, O God,
the work of my mind.
Bless to me, O God,
the work of my heart.

Anonymous

Surviving

Enemies are awful
and enemies are mean
but all their wicked, wicked deeds
by God above are seen.

Now God is all forgiving
but God is also good
and God will sort them out one day
just like I wish I could.

Dear God,
Give us the courage to overcome anger
with love.

Good deeds

Dear God,
When I see someone in trouble,
may I know when to stop and help
and when to hurry to fetch help;
but may I never pass by,
pretending I did not see.

Based on Jesus' parable of the Good Samaritan

Love is giving, not taking,
mending, not breaking,
trusting, believing,
never deceiving,
patiently bearing
and faithfully sharing
each joy, every sorrow,
today and tomorrow.

Anonymous

Endings

When little creatures die
And it's time to say goodbye
To a bright-eyed furry friend,
We know that God above
Will remember them with love:
A love that will never end.

Days are darker

The darkness comes:
Give thanks for the night.

The stars appear:
Give thanks for their light.

The air is still:
Give thanks for the calm.

And God is here:
Keep us safe from harm.

Winter

Now the wind is coming,
Now the wind is strong,
Now the winter freezes
And the darkness will be long.
Now we see the starlight
In the midnight sky,
We know God is with us
And the angels are close by.

Winter fun

Winter boots for puddles
Winter boots for snow
Winter boots for all the muddy places that I go.

Winter hats for chilly days
Winter hats for storms
Thank you, God, for winter clothes
   that help to keep us warm.

Feeling unwell

In my bed
and feeling rotten,
bored and gloomy
and forgotten.
May the angels
in the sky
watch to check
I do not die.
May the angels
here on land
come and hold me
by the hand.

A prayer for winter sniffles
A prayer for winter sneezes
A prayer said in a croaky voice
With little grunts and wheezes.

Changing seasons

O God,
You set the patterns of the seasons –
summer and winter,
seedtime and harvest –
so that all living things may flourish.

But we have been greedy
for warmth in wintertime
cool air in summertime
harvest crops at seedtime
spring flowers as the year grows old.

Teach us to live peaceably with the world.
Let the patterns be restored
and bless us.

Safe this night

Lord, keep us safe this night,
Secure from all our fears;
May angels guard us while we sleep,
Till morning light appears.

John Leland (1754–1841)

Now I lay me down to sleep,
I pray thee, Lord, thy child to keep;
Thy love to guard me through the night
And wake me in the morning light.

Traditional

Christmas

Let us travel to Christmas
By the light of a star.
Let us go to the hillside
Right where the shepherds are.
Let us see shining angels
Singing from heaven above.
Let us see Mary cradling
God's holy child with love.

For Jesus' sake

Lord, make me an instrument of your peace.

Where there is hatred, let me sow love;

Where there is injury, pardon;

Where there is discord, union;

Where there is doubt, faith;

Where there is despair, hope;

Where there is darkness, light;

Where there is sadness, joy;

For your mercy and your truth's sake.

Attributed to St Francis of Assisi (1181–1226)

Christmas love

At Christmas time,
the angels come
to earth from heaven above,
and God's gift to everyone
is the gift of love.

At Christmas time
the angels' song
is heard upon the ground,
as we share the gift of love
with everyone around.

May peace and plenty be the first
to lift the latch to your door,
and happiness be guided to your home
by the candle of Christmas.

Irish blessing

Easter

The autumn leaves were laid to rest
But now the trees are green,
And signs that God brings all to life
Throughout the world are seen.

And Jesus is alive, they say,
And death is not the end.
We rise again in heaven's light
With Jesus as our friend.

A friend of Jesus

Jesus, friend of little children,
Be a friend to me;
Take my hand, and ever keep me
Close to thee.

Walter J. Mathams (1851–1931)

Our Father in heaven,
hallowed be your name,
your kingdom come,
your will be done,
on earth as in heaven.
Give us today our daily bread.
Forgive us our sins
as we forgive those who sin against us.
Lead us not into temptation
but deliver us from evil.

The prayer Jesus taught

For the kingdom, the power,
and the glory are yours
now and for ever.

Amen

Resolutions

O God,
I will pray to you in the morning,
I will pray to you at sunrise.

I will ask you to show me the way that I should go.

I will ask you to protect me from the people
who do not like me, who want to hurt me.

I will trust in you to protect me,
I will trust in your love.

From Psalm 5

O God,
I will live this day thoughtfully so that, if my guardian angel were to give an account of it, I would not be ashamed.

Index of first lines